Snuff box made by C. Stiven of Laurencekirk, Aberdeenshire, in the first half of the nineteenth century. It measures 2¼ by 1¼ by ½ inches (5.7 by 3.2 by 1.3 cm), appreciably smaller than the illustration. Fasque, the subject on the snuff-box lid, was the home of Sir John Gladstone (1764–1851), a well known Liverpool merchant and father of William Ewart Gladstone (Prime Minister 1868–74, 1880–5, 1886 and 1892–4). Fasque is situated only a few miles from Laurencekirk, where the box was made. The base and sides of the box are in a predominantly yellow tartan decoration. This view has been recorded on other snuff boxes and may have been commissioned by Sir John Gladstone as a gift. It therefore seems possible that the equestrian figures are of Sir John and Lady Gladstone.

Mauchline Ware

and Associated Scottish Souvenir Ware

John Baker

A Shire book

Published in 2004 by Shire Publications Ltd,
Cromwell House, Church Street, Princes Risborough,
Buckinghamshire HP27 9AA, UK.
(Website: www.shirebooks.co.uk)

Copyright © 1985 and 2004 by John Baker.
First published 1985; reprinted 1991 and 1998. Second
edition, revised and illustrated in colour, 2004.
Shire Album 140. ISBN 0 7478 0581 4.
John Baker is hereby identified as the author of this work
in accordance with Section 77 of the Copyright, Designs
and Patents Act 1988.

British Library Cataloguing in Publication Data:
Baker, John. Mauchline ware and associated
Scottish souvenir ware. – 2nd ed. – (Shire album; 140)
1. Mauchline ware
2. Mauchline ware – History
3. Mauchline ware – Pictorial works
I. Title
745.5'94'09411
ISBN 0 7478 0581 4.

Cover: *Some of the vast range of both products and finishes crafted by the boxmakers of Ayrshire, mainly during the nineteenth century.*

ACKNOWLEDGEMENTS
Many of the people who provided such valuable assistance to the author at the first printing
of this book are, alas, no longer with us. It is invidious to mention survivors and more recent
helpers. Suffice it to say that without the help of many kind people in Mauchline and elsewhere
this book could not have been written.
Most of the photographs in this edition are the author's own efforts. However, those on pages
9 (centre), 14 (top), 16, 19 (top right), 28 (top right), 40 (centre), 41 (centre bottom), 42 (top right
and top left) and 44 (bottom) are the work of K. B. Photographics of Cheltenham. The
photographs on pages 8 (bottom), 9 (top), 15, 24 (centre), 29 (top left and top right), 30 (top), 44
(upper right) and 45 (top left and centre) were produced by Bob Rudge of Impact Photography
of Gloucester. Of these, those on pages 8 (bottom), 15 and 30 (top) are reproduced by kind
permission of BK Fine Art of Gloucester. William and Ruth Hodges kindly provided the
photographs on pages 10 (lower), 34 (lower) and 35 (lower). The illustration on page 20 (top left)
is reproduced by courtesy of Cheltenham Art Gallery and Museum.

Printed in Malta by Gutenberg Press Limited, Gudja Road,
Tarxien PLA 19, Malta.

Contents

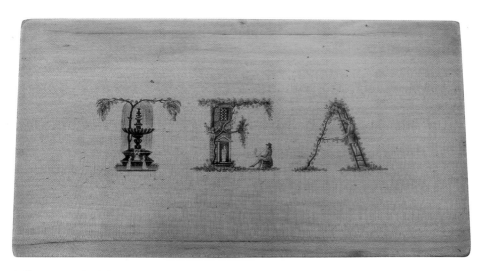

Delicate pen and ink decoration on a tea-caddy lid. Female workers at Smiths' Box Works received caddies like this as wedding gifts from their employers.

A fine oak snuff box measuring 4¹/₈ by 1¹/₂ by 1¹/₄ inches (10.5 by 3.8 by 3.2 cm), manufactured by C. Stiven of Laurencekirk. Few items of Mauchline ware can be accurately dated and this is one of those rarities. The caption within the silver cartouche reads: 'Presented by the Earl of Airlie to Mr MacDonald of Staffa on 17th Jan'y 1831, the box being made out of one of the oak joists of Airlie Castle which had been preserved at the time the Ancient Edifice was burnt down in 1693'. The site of Airlie Castle is only 4 miles (6 km) from Alyth, the home of James Sandy, who is credited with the invention of the integral (or hidden) hinge snuff box, of which this is an excellent example. Staffa is a small island now under the aegis of the National Trust for Scotland. It lies some 6 miles (10 km) west of the Isle of Mull and is best known for Fingal's Cave.

Introduction

Some 11 miles (18 km) inland from the Scottish coastal resort of Ayr lies the small town of Mauchline – pronounced 'Moch'lin'. When passing through the town today, it is difficult to appreciate that this was the centre of an industry that in its heyday in the 1860s employed some four hundred people in the manufacture of small but always beautifully made and invariably useful wooden souvenirs and gift ware. Not only were Mauchline's products sold throughout the United Kingdom but vast quantities were exported to many parts of Europe, North America, South Africa, Australia and probably elsewhere. Very similar products were made in other locations, notably Lanark, but so dominant was the contribution of

Cutty Sark. A scene from Robert Burns's 'Tam O'Shanter'. The Cutty Sark (a short skirt) refers to the scantily clad maiden holding centre stage as Tam, astride his mare Maggie, views 'an unco' sight!'. The box, measuring 3¹/₂ by 2¹/₈ by ³/₄ inches (8.8 by 5.4 by 1.9 cm), is stamped 'DAVID CRICHTON & CO. CUMNOCK'. The decoration is in penwork.

4

Four-in-hand coach. Another box by Crichton of Cumnock. This typical subject for snuff-box decoration is in pen and ink with some colour. The base and sides are painted black. The size is 4 by 1³/₄ by 1¹/₈ inches (10.1 by 4.4 by 2.9 cm).

the Mauchline firm of W. & A. Smith that, irrespective of the source of manufacture, the vast range of wooden souvenirs produced in south-west Scotland from the early years of the nineteenth century until the 1930s is now referred to by the generic name of 'Mauchline ware'.

If it were not for the town's association with Robert Burns it would be difficult to find any present-day connection with the industry that provided employment for the bulk of the town's workforce for over a century. Mauchline's Burns House Museum does, however, include an excellent collection of the products of W. & A. Smith as well as commemorating the local poet. The factory itself, known locally as the Box Works, was badly damaged by fire in 1933, this date effectively marking the end of production of the lines for which the firm was so well known. Ironically enough, the site is now occupied by the Mauchline fire station.

This fine snuff box by an unknown maker is curved to fit comfortably into a jacket pocket. The lid decoration, in pen and ink work, is another Burnsian inspired subject, the inscription reading 'Here are we met, three merry boys. Three merry boys I trow are we'. The base and sides are covered in an intricate thistle and leaf design. The box measures 3¹/₈ by 2 by ⁷/₈ inches (7.9 by 5.1 by 2.5 cm).

5

The origins

Above: *Another
snuff box by C.
Stiven of
Laurencekirk. It
measures 4 by 2¹/₈ by
1¹/₂ inches (10.1 by
5.4 by 3.8 cm). The
painting on the lid
depicting a hunting
scene is in full colour
and is of fine quality.
Although unsigned,
it is clearly the work
of a very competent
artist. The box is too
tall to fit into a
pocket and was
doubtless intended
for use on a side table
adjacent to a
comfortable chair!*

Mauchline ware developed partly by accident and partly through necessity. Towards the end of the eighteenth century in the town of Alyth, Perth & Kinross, there lived a man of remarkable inventiveness by the name of James Sandy. Sandy, who died in 1819 at the age of fifty-three, had for much of his life been bedridden. Among his many achievements was the invention of the 'hidden-hinge' snuff box was the most important. The knuckles of the snuff box's hinge were formed alternately from the lid and the back of the box, with a metal rod passing very precisely through the centre of the knuckles. This rod was a little shorter than the box so as not to protrude through the ends, which were then 'stopped' with a minute plug in such a way that the mechanism was invisible even on close inspection. However, the manufacture and marketing of this invention was left to Charles Stiven from Laurencekirk, Aberdeenshire, the product being initially referred to as the Laurencekirk snuff box.

The wood used was generally sycamore, which has a very close grain and a pleasing colour. Early snuff boxes were hand-decorated either in coloured paints or in pen and ink work. The finished boxes were then given numerous coats of varnish, which enriched the final appearance as well as protecting the surface. Highly skilled artists were employed in this work, including the well known Victorian watercolourist William Leighton Leitch, who later became one of Queen Victoria's tutors. Favourite subjects for snuff-box decoration were coaching scenes, field sports and 'drinking' topics.

By some means, but certainly not by design, the secret of the hidden-hinge snuff box found its way to Cumnock in East Ayrshire, only a few miles from Mauchline. The first manufacturer in Cumnock was William Crawford around 1810. Whether he copied the Laurencekirk hinge from a box brought to him for repair, or not, we may never know for certain, although this does seem a plausible explanation and is the one now generally accepted. Crawford was unable to keep the secret to himself for very long, because by the

Diagram illustrating how the knuckles of the integral hidden-hinge snuff box are formed alternately from the lid and back of the box.

early 1820s at least fifty separate Scottish snuff-box manufacturers are known to have existed, mainly in Ayrshire. These included William and Andrew Smith of Mauchline, whose family had previously been employed in the production of razor hones in the locality.

With so many manufacturers, total snuff-box production was considerable but the habit of snuff taking was beginning to decline. It became essential for manufacturers to diversify in order to survive. This was beyond the capabilities of many of the specialist snuff-box manufacturers, who eventually went out of business, thereby reducing competition for the survivors, one of whom was W. & A. Smith. However, according to an account of the economy of Mauchline published in 1845, the town possessed a 'very extensive manufactory of wooden snuff boxes. In this work about sixty people are employed, who work ten hours a day, six days per week.' It seems most unlikely that production could have been limited to snuff boxes for so long and the probability is that other items were also being made, although the firm was still mainly known for its original products. This view is strengthened by a report only five years later in the *Art Journal* in which Andrew Smith himself stated that the products of his firm 'now consist of every article which you can almost conceive it possible to make, from postage stamp boxes up to tea trays'.

The first of the 'new' products were tea caddies utilising the remarkable hidden hinge, tea being an expensive commodity, which, like snuff, benefited from being kept in an airtight container. It is said that on marriage female employees of Smiths' Box Works were presented with one of the firm's tea caddies. This was a more generous gift than it may seem because these caddies were expensive items, being beautifully decorated and most skilfully made.

Over the course of the next century Smiths of Mauchline and their few competitors were to produce tens of thousands of articles in hundreds of styles and in several different finishes, selling them in virtually every inhabited location in Scotland and many cities, towns and villages in England and Wales, and with a considerable export market.

Snuff boxes continued to be made, albeit in ever decreasing numbers, well into the 1870s and at least one Smiths' employee possessed the necessary skills to repair damaged boxes into the twentieth century. The invention and development of the hidden-hinge snuff box is therefore a vital part of the history of Mauchline ware, without which the fascinating range of beautifully produced items, now sought after by an ever increasing number of collectors throughout the world, would never have been created.

The product range

Since most Mauchline ware items were produced in at least two and very often three or four different finishes it is logical to consider the range of products before dealing with the various types of decoration.

From the 1830s a steadily decreasing number of snuff boxes continued to be made alongside an ever increasing range of needlework, stationery, domestic and cosmetic items as well as articles for personal decoration and amusement. In addition an incredible range of boxes in every conceivable shape and size and for limitless purposes was also produced. Tea caddies, cigar cases and visiting-card cases were among the first of the new lines but by the middle of the century, when the industry was at its zenith, virtually anything that could be produced in wood, was

A packed display of a wide variety of items, most of which are decorated with transfer prints. A number of these pieces appear in more detail in other illustrations.

A fine tea caddy decorated with the word 'TEA' in delicate penwork (shown on page 3), together with its two tea containers and a delightful inkwell holder in the form of a boat. The boat includes two 'holds' for pen nibs and brass rowlocks to secure the oars, which are pen holders. Both boat and oars carry Eastbourne transfer-print decorations. Inkwell holders were produced in numerous shapes and in all the main finishes.

A group of five cotton or thread containers in various non-standard finishes. All were made for the Paisley company of Clark & Co, who purchased vast numbers of similar containers for their wares. Other manufacturers of similar products were also good customers of the Mauchline ware producers.

comparatively small and served a useful purpose found its way into the product range.

Needlework items are the most numerous group. Containers designed to house or dispense cottons, threads, silks, ribbons, wool, string, pins and needles were made in many shapes and sizes. Also produced were darning blocks and mushrooms, scissors cases, containers for knitting pins, crochet hooks and bodkins and a remarkable range of novelty thimble containers and tape measures. Among the most attractive sewing items are the delightful egg-shaped sewing 'etuis', varying in size from bantam to duck egg.

These eggs, when opened, reveal a hollow dowel with a removable top fixed to the base of the egg and designed to hold needles. A small cotton or thread spool was passed over the dowel and a thimble completed these delightful portable sewing companions.

A large number of cotton, thread and ribbon manufacturers purchased Mauchline ware containers for their

Right: Darning 'mushrooms'. The bottle shape carries a transfer view of Herne Bay, Kent. The others (from left to right) have views of Largs, North Ayrshire, from the pier, and the Wish Tower, Eastbourne, East Sussex; both are transfer views. Blackpool Tower, Lancashire, is in photographic ware.

Left: A group of thimble holders, all of which are in the form of miniature knife boxes. (From left to right) Tynemouth, Northumberland, transfer print; black lacquer with floral decoration to the top; The Arcade, Birmingham, transfer print; Stuart tartan; Laxey Wheel, Isle of Man, transfer print.

9

Visiting-card cases. The left-hand example is in sea-flower decoration, the middle one is transfer-printed with a view of the Wallace Monument, Abbey Craig, Stirling, and the one on the right is in Lorne tartan ware. The lid of the tartan example simply lifts off. The viewer will note the small gold marker on the top part of the case, just above the word 'Lorne' (difficult to make out, on the main body of the case). If the lid were replaced the wrong way round, the tartan design would not match up. The other cases incorporate a neat metal hinge that allows the top part to swivel around to facilitate opening and closing.

Razor strops were among the earliest products. These two strops were the property of William Wilson (1865–1944), the last works manager of W. & A. Smith's Mauchline Box Works. Between the strops is a closed fan, the sticks of which are in coloured fern decoration.

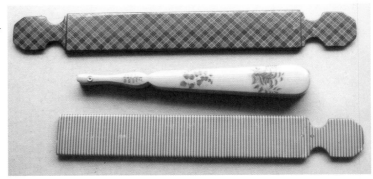

Cribbage scorers. The top example is in Prince Charlie tartan. The scorer in the middle is in fern ware and carries the message 'A souvenir from Weymouth' (Dorset). The very appealing lower scorer is in a most unusual finish, panelled with green imitation marble with a central floral strip. The four pins (two in red and two in white) are to be found in all such scorers and are housed in receiving holes (two at each end) and held in by means of a brass swivel plate, here just discernible.

products, their names being clearly yet discreetly displayed either inside the lid or on the base. Thus rather mundane necessities were transformed into attractive gifts. Manufacturers known to have used Mauchline ware boxes in this way include J. & P. Coates, Clarks, Chadwicks, Glenfield, Kerr, MEQ and Medlock.

Although W. & A. Smith were very prominent, they were not without competitors. Perhaps the most significant of these was the Caledonian Box Works, which was established in Lanark by the very enterprising Archibald Brown. The Lanark works opened in 1866, some four years after Brown's marriage in Mauchline, where he is recorded as being a box manufacturer. It is possible that he may have spent a brief period working for W. & A. Smith. Brown's product range at the new works was not dissimilar to Smiths' at Mauchline and, by all accounts, his also became a sizeable and highly successful enterprise. He was a very keen photographer (see 'Photographic ware') and in the last few years of his life he devoted more of his time to this interest than to the box works. He secured large orders from firms such as J. & P. Coates, the cotton and thread manufacturers, for attractively designed boxes to house the firm's products. These required eyelets through which to pass the cotton or thread, and the bone from which these were made was supplied by the local abattoir, with which Brown had a contract. Doubtless, similar boxes were made for other cotton and thread producers.

Stationery items ranged in size from large blotting folders down to small bookmarks and included cylindrical rulers in great variety, some incorporating a pencil and rubber while others were covered in a mass of postal information. Rulers containing rubbers and pencils are instantly recognisable by a small knob at one end for the pencil and a much larger knob for the rubber at the other end. If the knobs are of uniform size it is unlikely that the ruler has any additional facility. Novelty inkwells, pens, pencils, pencil boxes and letter openers were also made, as well as many designs of bookmark, including a patented combined bookmark and paper cutter.

Boxes were produced for postage stamps of one, two or three denominations, and the single-denomination boxes were usually

Letter openers and combined bookmarks/page-cutters. One letter opener is in Prince Charlie tartan and another is in coloured fern ware. The two bookmarks/page-cutters are in M'Beth tartan and 'forget-me-not' floral decoration.

Desk equipment. (From top to bottom) Pen tray with two transfer-printed views of Great Yarmouth, Norfolk; a square-section 'continuous' rubber, the rubber being pushed through as it is used; a pen holder; and an unsharpened pencil. The last three items are all in unnamed tartan decoration.

circular. The larger boxes were fitted with 'slopes' to facilitate easy stamp removal. Tartan-finished boxes often had a facsimile stamp or even a genuine one glued to the lid. The head of Sir Rowland Hill, the originator of the Penny Post, will be found decorating some stamp boxes.

Although wood is perhaps not the most obvious material for making items of personal decoration, a number of very attractive bracelets, earrings and brooches were produced in Mauchline ware. Some of the bracelets incorporated hand-painted segments suggesting manufacture around or perhaps before 1860. Such items would have been expensive.

The most beautiful and delicate handles were made for ladies' parasols and, since gloves were an essential part of Victorian dress, glove stretchers were another requirement produced in Mauchline ware. Accessories for the dressing table included ring trees and powder-puff boxes as well as clothes brushes and hairbrushes. One of the most unusual items recorded in this group is a posy holder,

Items for personal adornment. The seven brooches include: transfer-printed views of Corby Castle, Cumbria, and Fyvie Cottage Hospital (Fyvie is in Aberdeenshire, some 8 miles, or 13 km, south of Turriff); the well known Nasmyth portrait of Robert Burns; two portrait profiles in surrounds of unspecified tartans; and two 'doughnut' brooches in M'Innes tartan (top) and Malcolm tartan. The bracelet comprises seven segments, six in tartan and the larger segment decorated with a painted view of Loch Vennacher.

A group of novelty measuring tapes. (From left to right) Bottle shape with transfer view of the pier, Walton on the Naze, Essex; butter churn with transfer view of the Liffey, Custom House and Eden Quay, Dublin; bell with photographic view of Gray Head (this is possibly intended to be Grey Head, Orkney); cylinder shape showing Adelaide Terrace, Portishead, near Bristol; lighthouse shape depicting Grange (there are several locations in the British Isles with this name but the example is possibly in Cumbria).

possibly derived from the more common tulip-shaped spill vase. Containers for cosmetics included boxes designed for face powder, rouge, cold cream and lipsalve.

The domestic scene was very well catered for, napkin rings being perhaps the most common item of all. They were made in all Mauchline ware finishes and were also among the lines produced from relatively early days until the end of production in the 1930s. They will often be found numbered from one to six, having originally formed part of a boxed set. Occasionally rings numbered up to twelve will also be found.

The Victorian breakfast table may well have been graced by a Mauchline ware egg-cup cruet although individual egg cups are far more likely to be found by collectors. Several versions of egg timers, both free-standing and for wall mounting, were also produced.

Items of more general usage include a wide variety of spill vases and candlesticks. These were made in all the main finishes as well as more costly versions produced from two contrasting woods.

Matches were essential to the Victorian home and a wide range of match containers was manufactured. Some were no more than novelty matchboxes serving no additional purpose, while others incorporated a bone holder for an individual match. Often erroneously called 'go-to-beds', this type could serve the purpose of a candle providing light for just long enough to get into bed. Their true purpose, however, was to melt sealing wax without burning one's fingers!

Money boxes. (Back) Locomotive, The Parade, Skegness, Lincolnshire. (Middle row, from left to right) Castle, Great Malvern, Worcestershire; chest, Melrose Abbey, Scottish Borders; cottage, Pevensey Castle, East Sussex. (Front) 'Trick' money box, West Bay, Bridport, Dorset. All are in transfer ware.

Containers for money ranged from ladies' handbags, a tartan ware version being owned by Queen Victoria, and smaller purses through to a massive range of money boxes. Some money boxes are in the form of chests and castles but an unusual shape is that of a locomotive. Trick money boxes were produced and are generally found either in almost mint condition, indicating that the young saver had despaired of extracting his or her money and given up trying, or in a very poor state, where youthful patience has been exhausted and various implements have been used as safe-cracking tools!

At least three distinct versions of spectacle cases have been recorded, and the interest in photography is catered for with picture frames in many styles and sizes as well as Mauchline ware boarded photograph albums.

These three playing-card boxes all have transfer-print decoration in addition to the three facsimile playing cards that indicate the boxes' purpose. Such boxes will also be found in other finishes. In each of these examples a representative from the suit of Hearts is absent! Card boxes, as in these examples, were generally made to receive two packs of playing cards, although larger boxes exist. The lower box will accommodate two packs of cards horizontally side by side, while the other examples incorporate a division so that the packs are held vertically side by side.

Some of the items auctioned by Bruton Knowles at their Cheltenham salerooms in June 1997. Of special note are the unusual domed fern ware workbox, the black lacquer box (centre of picture), which originally held six cotton reels and also incorporated a game of fortunes, and the rare cheroot case with a penwork illustration of a rowing crew, all named. Other items include snuff boxes and pin wheels.

The Victorians were great card players and this interest is represented by boxes for one, two or even more packs of playing cards. Usually these boxes had three miniature cards glued to the top to indicate their purpose. Other items associated with games include cribbage boards, bezique markers, dice shakers and Chinese puzzles.

A small circular tartan box with three minute cards on the lid contains four black lacquer discs. A small facsimile card, one for each suit, appears on the reverse of each disc to indicate which suit is trumps.

The children were not ignored and skipping-rope handles, tops, pop guns and whistles will all be found in Mauchline ware.

There remains one great puzzle. This concerns the 'Breadalbane' button, or rather the tens of thousands of these buttons believed to have been made from the late 1840s until the early 1850s. Originally produced for the nobleman after whom they were named, production was said to have reached twelve thousand daily at one stage! Victorian buttons have survived in vast numbers and yet relatively few Breadalbane buttons have come to light, although those that have are in good condition. Perhaps an explanation for their puzzling scarcity will one day be found.

This chapter is by no means exhaustive but gives the reader some indication of the vast range of items produced in Mauchline ware during its hundred or so years of manufacture. The following chapters deal with the various finishes applied to these products.

Transfer ware

The precise date of the first transfer-printed wares is not known but they were certainly being manufactured in quantity by the early 1850s and possibly very much earlier, continuing until the effective end of Mauchline ware production in 1933. More items were produced with transfer decoration than in any other finish. Transfer ware was true souvenir ware in that each piece was decorated with a view associated with the place of purchase.

The transfers were applied to the finished articles prior to their receiving several coats of slow-drying oil copal varnish. This process was said to take from six to twelve weeks to complete, although it seems certain that accelerated means of varnishing must have been developed to cope with the sheer scale of production. However, this lengthy and careful process of manufacture must largely account for the extreme durability of these products, many of which have survived in near mint condition.

As with the earlier hand-decorated snuff boxes, the main type of wood used continued to be sycamore, generally known as 'plane' in Scotland, its pale colour making an excellent foil for the darker transfers. While the majority of Mauchline ware items were small, thus warranting only a single transfer, it was by no means unusual for six or even more transfers to be applied to some larger pieces. Where more than one transfer was applied, the views were always related to one another, either by subject or else geographically.

Whistles. (Top) Combined whistle and pop gun, Blackgang Chine, Isle of Wight (transfer). (Centre) George Square, Glasgow (transfer). (Lower, left to right) The lighthouse, Cromer, Norfolk (transfer); HMS Foudroyant (photographic); The Cupee, Sark, Channel Islands (transfer).

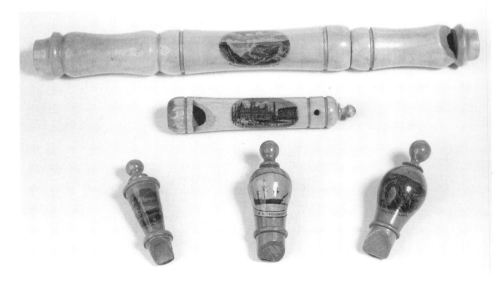

Photograph frame, 5¼ by 3¾ inches (13.3 by 9.5 cm), sold by Mr W. Brand of Wooler, a small Northumberland town about 15 miles (24 km) from the Scottish border. All of the four transfer-printed views depict locations within a few miles of Wooler, noted to this day for the nearby Chillingham herd of white cattle. The subject of the photograph is Mrs Euphemia ('Effie') Smith, née Wilson (1899–1984), whose father, William Wilson (1865–1944), was the last works manager of W. & A. Smith of Mauchline. Effie, who was a great source of information to the author, worked as a packer at the firm from 1918 until the fire of 1933.

The Scottish home market appears to have been completely saturated. While 'Burnsian' views form by far the largest single grouping and views associated with Sir Walter Scott also figure prominently, there can hardly be a location in Scotland that was not recorded. In addition to virtually every town and village, a vast number of beauty spots, country houses, churches, schools, ruins and even cottage hospitals have been immortalised in transfer ware. The remainder of Great Britain was hardly less well represented, although views were in the main of the many seaside resorts and inland spa towns that became increasingly accessible to a growing number of people as a result of the rapidly expanding rail network.

The Isle of Wight was particularly well catered for, possibly because of Queen Victoria's love of the island through her residence

Ann Hathaway's Cottage, near Stratford-upon-Avon, Warwickshire.

George Stephenson's 'Locomotion', the first locomotive to be used on a public railway.

at Osborne House, itself the subject of transfer views. Each of the popular south and east coast resorts, including Bournemouth, Brighton, Eastbourne, Hastings, Margate, Clacton and Scarborough, was represented with several views. Neither did the Channel Islands escape the attention of the Mauchline ware manufacturers, and even Sark, with its tiny population, warranted at least one view, while the main islands of Jersey and Guernsey are very well recorded. The ever popular Stratford-upon-Avon was a close rival to London's many places of interest, although some of the capital's most obvious landmarks seem not to have been recorded. Among the many inland resorts featured in transfer views are Harrogate, Chester, Bath, Malvern and Cheltenham. Inevitably some less obvious places were recorded, possibly because an anticipated tourist boom failed to materialise. This would account for views of Torrington Station or the New Baths at Croft!

Since transfer ware was produced continuously for some eighty years it is reasonable to assume that there would have been periodic updating at least of urban views to reflect changes of fashion, transport and indeed of the towns themselves. The evidence, however, is to the contrary. New transfers were introduced as more and more places were considered sufficiently commercial, but there is no clear evidence of an earlier view being revised. From the mid 1890s motorised transport became increasingly commonplace but although a great many town and city scenes have been recorded remarkably few views have come to light showing any form of motorised transport. Indeed, railways are as old as transfer ware itself and yet locomotives appear on only a handful of views. This suggests that most of the transfer plates were made before about 1880, with few, if any, being produced after 1890. Although production was to continue for another forty years or so the popularity of Mauchline ware was in decline and the cost of producing a vast number of new plates would perhaps have been prohibitive.

Since the same or similar transfer ware views were used over a long period, they are of little assistance in dating any

Holyrood Palace, Edinburgh.

Transfer-printed Welsh market scene applied to a black lacquer box.

This transfer-printed view of High Street, Mauchline, East Ayrshire, decorates the top of a miniature three-legged stool incorporating a pincushion. The wood is said to have been grown in Gavin Hamilton's garden.

Scarborough Aquarium, North Yorkshire. This view is on the top of a cylindrical reel holder.

Above: *High Street, Bridgnorth, Shropshire.*

Left: *Transfer-printed view of the Old Market Cross, Wakefield, West Yorkshire. It is on the base of a circular stamp box.*

19

Stamp box for two denominations of postage stamp. The transfer print is of the Grammar School, Cheltenham, Gloucestershire, demolished in the 1960s.

Circular pin disc with transfer view of St Paul's Cathedral, London.

Heart-shaped pin holder with view of Isambard Kingdom Brunel's Clifton Suspension Bridge, Bristol – road, rail and sea transport, all on one view!

Note tablet with metal clasp fastener and transfer view of the Promenade Drive, Cheltenham, Gloucestershire.

particular piece. This difficulty is aggravated by the fact that so many lines such as napkin rings, paper knives, rulers, egg cups and memo books were themselves produced in very similar form throughout the transfer ware era.

There are, however, exceptions. A large number of books were produced with Mauchline ware boards. Many carry a publication date and others, especially those purchased as gifts, often have a dated inscription on the flyleaf.

A number of major exhibitions and royal occasions were commemorated with transfer views so that articles so decorated can be very accurately dated. Exhibitions were held in Glasgow in 1861 and in Edinburgh in 1886, the venues of both being recorded by transfer views.

Box with transfer view of Barnstaple, Devon. It is, in effect, a view of the town's railway station.

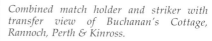

Combined match holder and striker with transfer view of Buchanan's Cottage, Rannoch, Perth & Kinross.

Below: *Circular box depicting the Victoria Hotel and the entrance to the pier, Southport, Lancashire.*

Below: *Transfer-printed view of West Bay, Bridport, Dorset. This object, a trick money box, is in the collection of Bridport Museum.*

Queen Victoria's Golden Jubilee of 1887 was a fillip for the Mauchline ware manufacturers, with a wide range of goods celebrating this event with transfer decorations. Probably the last royal occasion to receive this treatment was the coronation of King George V in 1911.

Occasionally a less orthodox form of dating is possible. For example, the child's money box in the form of a castle (illustrated on page 14), in fine condition and decorated with a view of Malvern in Worcestershire, still contains a note from the original donor. It reads: 'For Mary Selina Badham, born Thursday, July 2nd 1886 being one penny per week from the date of her birth, from her Aunt and Godmother, Elizabeth Tidman.' The fact that the box was in near mint condition well over a century later, complete with note (but no pennies!), initially suggested the likelihood of Mary's death in infancy. However, subsequent research by a Mauchline Ware Collectors Club member revealed that Mary had married, although she had no family, and had died in Bristol in 1978 at the grand age of ninety-two! Another example is a small crayon box with a view of Glasgow Royal Exchange, proudly inscribed as belonging to Maggie Todd of Newlands, Glasgow, and dated 1897. But, for the most part,

Advertising letter opener from W. & A. Smith. One side lists many of the firm's products while the reverse (shown below) gives the current (1890s) postal information. The handle portion carries transfer views of Burns Cottage at Alloway, South Ayrshire, and Edinburgh Castle.

An unusual stamp box for two denominations of postage stamp, in the form of a drawer. The transfer view is of Castle Street, Aberdeen.

Letter or postcard container with illustration of the Proprietary College, Cheltenham, Gloucestershire, now known as Cheltenham College.

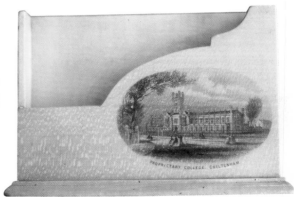

POSTAL INFORMATION.

INLAND TELEGRAMS.
Sixpence for first 12 Words, and a Half-penny for each additional word.

LETTER POST.
4 oz., 1d ; 6 oz., 1½d ; 8 oz., 2d ; and so on at the Rate of ½d for every additional 2 oz.

PARCEL POST.
1 lb., 3d ; 2 lbs., 4d ; 3 lbs., 5d ; 4 lbs., 6d ; 5 lbs., 7d ; 6 lbs., 8d ; 7 lbs., 9d ; 8 lbs., 10d ; 9 lbs., 11d ; 10 and 11 lbs., 1s.

POSTAL ORDERS.
1/ and 1/6 ; ½d ; 2/, 2/6, 3/, 3/6, 4/, 4/6, 5/, 7/6, 10/, and 10/6, 1d ; 15/ and 20/, 1½d.

BOOK POST.
Postage for 2 oz. that weight are tre

NEWSPAPERS.
The Prepaid Posta Inland Newspaper

A small box decorated with a view of St Mary's Church, Eastbourne, East Sussex.

Views of London are far less common than one might expect. However, they do exist and this and the following view are on the two 'boards' of a swivel-type memorandum tablet. The first view is of Holborn Viaduct.

The second view shows Blackfriars New Bridge with both steam and sailing boats on the river. The dome of St Paul's cathedral is just visible in the left background.

The reverse of W. & A. Smith's advertising letter opener, illustrated above.

23

Inveraray Castle and Duniquaich, Argyll & Bute. The subject is a box that operates on the 'drawer' principal. It carries the name of John Rose, Postmaster, Inveraray, who is referred to as the 'publisher' – meaning that he was the retailer.

Right: 'The Birthday Oracle', published by William P. Nimmo of Edinburgh in 1883. This copy is inscribed 'Maggie House, July 13th 1885'. The transfer-printed cover view is of the Wallace Monument, Abbey Craig, Stirling, and the attractive design on the back states that the book was 'Bought in the Douglas Room of the Royal Palace, Stirling'.

Below: High Street, Biggar, South Lanarkshire. This transfer view decorates the front cover of 'The Language of Flowers', published by George Routledge & Sons of London.

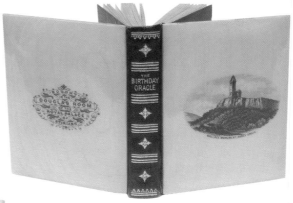

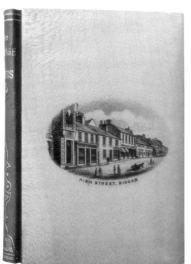

dating must be speculation based on the 'feel' that is acquired from handling a large number of different items.

Very occasionally a piece of transfer ware will additionally – and in very small print – include a 'publisher's name'. This refers to the name of the retailer and probably indicates a particularly prolific selling agent. The name of C. Maclean or Maclean & Son of Dundalk has been frequently recorded, the Maclean family having been stationers in that town prior to 1911. John Rose was postmaster at Inveraray around 1880 and his name appears on some items depicting the well known local castle. A. & R. Robb are also recorded at Coldstream, where they had a grocer's and newsagent's business towards the end of the nineteenth century. These 'publisher's names' probably appear on no more than one piece in a

A fine panoramic transfer view showing the town and sea front at Llandudno, Conwy (on a small box).

LLANDUDNO.

PARADE, TUNBRIDGE WELLS. Nº 2

Left: *Transfer-printed view of The Parade, Tunbridge Wells, Kent (now known as the Pantiles). It is marked 'No. 2', suggesting that there were companion views. The print is on a stamp box.*

hundred and are therefore well worth looking for.

Far more common was the practice of disclosing the source of the wood from which the article is purported to have been made. One 'stool' pin holder states that it was made from wood grown in Gavin Hamilton's garden. This piece is particularly interesting as the view is of Mauchline's High Street and Gavin Hamilton was a patron of Robert Burns. Other items were supposedly made from wood grown on Flodden Field, on the lands at Abbotsford, on the banks of the Doon or Tweed and even from the Old Gallows Tree at Doune Castle.

Photographic ware

Many items of Mauchline ware are found with photographs applied as a decoration as an alternative to transfer-printed views.

Although photographic ware was probably introduced some twenty to thirty years after the first transfer-printed items, examples will be found on most of the Mauchline ware product range. The obvious exceptions are snuff boxes, tea caddies and other early products, manufacture of which had virtually ceased by the time the first photographic ware came on to the market in the mid 1860s.

The commencement date may well have coincided with the establishment of the Caledonian Box Works in Lanark in 1866. Archibald Brown, its founder, was a keen photographer who is said to have made his own cameras. W. & A. Smith were at the height of their success at that time and it seems unlikely that Brown would have started his own factory in Lanark unless he had some new products in mind. Simply to compete with the long established Smiths by producing very similar wares would have been both unimaginative and probably commercially suicidal, and all the evidence suggests that Archibald Brown was nothing if not imaginative. It also seems possible that Brown was an acquaintance of the renowned George Washington Wilson, perhaps Scotland's best-known photographer. Wilson's work was used extensively on photographic ware and it seems possible that Brown, perhaps with the technical assistance of Wilson, had photographic decoration in mind when he started the Lanark company.

It is always difficult to date items of Mauchline ware with any accuracy but a copy of Sir Walter Scott's *The Lady of the Lake* is very helpful in this respect. The covers are in oak, not the more usual sycamore (or plane), and an inscription on the back board tells us that the book was bought in the Douglas Room at Stirling Castle. This

A photographic view of soldiers on the battlements of Stirling Castle, which appears on the oak covers of a copy, dated 1868, of Scott's 'The Lady of the Lake'.

This view of Ventnor, Isle of Wight, is still readily recognisable. Note the bathing machines.

Left: *Central Beach and New Band Stand, Herne Bay, Kent, a popular resort on the coast between Whitstable and Margate. This view decorates one end of an egg-timer.*

Below: *Sand yachts are clearly not a new idea. This late-nineteenth-century view of the beach at Southport, Lancashire, shows such a device with wheels with a diameter equal to the height of the man on the left.*

inscription appears on many items of Mauchline ware, suggesting that the castle was a very good retail outlet. The cover photograph shows in some detail a group of soldiers at ease on the battlements of Stirling Castle and is almost certainly the work of Wilson, to whom other photographs within the book are clearly attributed. While the book lacks a publication date, the original owner very helpfully dated the flyleaf, 8th July 1868. This is just two years after Archibald Brown started his Lanark manufactory and strengthens the view that photographic ware started about this time.

Most photographs found on Mauchline ware are of reasonably good quality, some being quite exceptional, and from a historical viewpoint are of far greater interest than transfer views since they are factual. However, some are somewhat indistinct, and

A Shetland knitter. This was once a common sight in the Northern Isles and doubtless other remote areas. The woman wastes no time in transporting a wicker basket laden with peat as she continues with her knitting. This photograph decorates a 'book' type needle wallet.

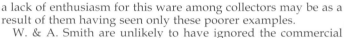

Scarborough Castle, North Yorkshire, from the harbour. The fishing boats are clear enough but the castle is no more than a distant shape. This view is on a small cylindrical container.

a lack of enthusiasm for this ware among collectors may be as a result of them having seen only these poorer examples.

W. & A. Smith are unlikely to have ignored the commercial potential of this new style of finish – assuming that it was first produced at Lanark – and there is little doubt that they too produced wares with photographic decoration.

Archibald Brown died at the comparatively young age of fifty-eight in 1891, his business having been run by two ex-employees,

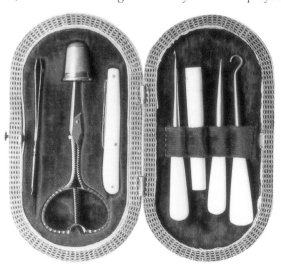

'From the Land of Burns'. This delightful family photograph (above) decorates the lid of a comprehensively equipped travelling companion (seen open in the picture on the right). This was clearly a special commission to one of the Mauchline ware makers. Perhaps several were made, to be given to family and friends. The style of dress suggests a late-nineteenth-century date.

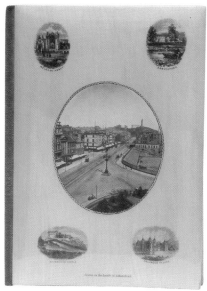

Above: *This box carries a superb photograph of the Falls of Clyde at Lanark, South Lanarkshire. The box was made at Archibald Brown's Caledonian Box Works at Lanark and his signature may just be discernible in the bottom right-hand corner. Charles Chislett, a local chemist, commissioned such boxes to contain his Falls of Clyde Bouquet products. The box measures 4½ by 3 inches (11.4 by 7.6 cm).*

Right: *This correspondence folder measures 9 by 6¼ inches (22.8 by 15.9 cm). It combines a fine photograph of Princes Street, Edinburgh, with four transfer prints of nearby landmarks. Many items of Mauchline ware are to be found with similar combinations of decoration. The high quality of the photograph can be judged by the enlargement (below right) of the road junction, centre left. The stepping stones against the kerb are clearly visible.*

William Mackenzie and John Meikle, since the late 1880s. In 1907 the Lanark works were sold, leaving W. & A. Smith as the sole large-scale manufacturer of Scottish souvenir woodware in south-west Scotland until they too ceased making such products in the 1930s.

Examples of Mauchline ware will be found combining a photograph or photographs with one or more transfer prints, and photographs will also be found associated with most other styles. All recorded photographic ware suggests that the period of manufacture was between the mid 1860s and the early years of the twentieth century. However, there is no evidence that photographic views were ever updated despite the many changes that took place during this forty-year period.

Tartan ware

In the early 1840s the inventive Smiths designed an ingenious machine capable of 'weaving' tartan designs on to paper. The machine employed a series of pens, each using a different coloured ink, the result being an accurate representation of the so-called authentic tartans.

Before this invention, tartan and plaid decoration was applied directly on to the wooden surface. This process required not only considerable skill and patience but also a vast amount of time, and without the new machine the production of tartan ware might well have been extremely short-lived. As it was, this finish became tremendously popular, not only in Scotland and the rest of Great Britain but also in other countries.

Many Mauchline ware items such as wool holders, egg cups, parasol handles and in particular the egg-shaped sewing companions have rounded surfaces and very great care was necessary in gluing tartan-printed paper to such articles. In theory it is impossible to apply material such as paper to a curved surface without obvious folds or joins. This difficulty was overcome,

(Top) A pair of scissors sheaths: M'Pherson tartan (left); M'Duff tartan (right). (Centre) An unsharpened pencil. (Bottom) A fine and delicate parasol handle in Frazer tartan.

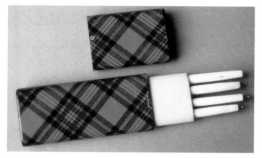

Above left: *Set of four crochet hooks in a Clan Stuart case. Note the location mark on the lid, which must line up with the tartan name to ensure a precise fit and a design match.*

Above right: *A rare sliding-lid container in Stuart tartan to hold four dice. Note that each is stamped with the royal (GR) cypher.*

however, by the application of black paint to areas where joins would occur, the joins being further disguised by the use of a wavy gold line. Similar care was exercised in matching the tartan design on articles comprising more than one part. So skilfully was this done that it is almost impossible for the naked eye to detect exactly where the parts meet.

The manufacturers stamped the name of the tartan on each product, with the exception of the smallest pieces such as buttons and cuff links. This was always done most unobtrusively in very small gold lettering on a black background.

A pair of Stuart tartan book covers or boards, probably intended to grace small books or needlecases. They measure 3½ by 2⅜ inches (8.9 by 6.3 cm). Although the views are both of Loch Katrine, Stirling, close examination reveals a number of differences, confirming them to be individual works.

Paper knife in the form of a penknife. It is in Caledonia tartan and is 3 inches (7.6 cm) in length. The blade is made of bone.

Lid of a circular stamp box designed for receipt stamps. It is in M'Inroy tartan and measures 2 inches (5.1 cm) in diameter.

Circular stamp box with the head of Prince Albert. It is in Caledonia tartan and is 1¾ inches (4.4 cm) in diameter.

Items of tartan ware are more likely to be found with the names M'Beth, M'Lean, M'Pherson and so on spelt in this fashion (i.e with an apostrophe following the capital M) than in the currently more common forms McBeth, McLean, McPherson (or MacBeth, MacLean, MacPherson). However, the latter forms will be found, although less frequently.

William and Andrew Smith took the accuracy of their tartan work very seriously. Indeed, they published their own version of *The Tartans of the Clans and Families of Scotland*, a publication consisting of an index of the sixty-nine 'authentic' tartans followed by a sample of each. This is one of very few books published by the Smiths although tartan-covered boards were used by many other publishers, especially for the works of Robert Burns and Sir Walter Scott.

Tartan decoration was applied to virtually the entire range of Mauchline ware products and its use continued into the twentieth century. However, a fire destroyed their patented tartan printing machine and later pieces were decorated

A double-ended pincushion (or needle cleaner) in Louise tartan with registration 'diamond', together with a similar item carrying a Christmas message.

32

'Doughnut' type brooch with a 'shield' applied to the centre. The illustration is of Holyrood Palace, Edinburgh, and the tartan is Stuart.

Sewing egg (etui) in M'Beth tartan. Cotton reels, needles and thimble are held in one delightful container.

in paper produced by an outside manufacturer. The quality of this paper and also of the later workmanship was distinctly inferior, and such items are easily recognised. Even the joins are clearly visible. Tartan ware was not made exclusively by the Smiths of Mauchline, although they produced the greater part. Davidson, Wilson & Amphlet, also of Mauchline, produced tartan ware, as did Archibald Brown's Caledonian Box Works in Lanark from the mid 1860s.

An eight-sided container for housing needle packets. The tartan is M'Pherson and the top is decorated with a gundog painting.

Fern ware

It used to be thought that fern ware was a last attempt to revive an industry in decline. However, there is now evidence that the earliest fern-decorated items date from about 1870, when the established transfer and tartan wares were still in great demand.

Fern ware was produced in smaller quantities than the other main finishes and it seems that three, if not four, different processes were used. Almost certainly the first fern ware was produced by W. & A. Smith, although it was also manufactured in Lanark at the Caledonian Box Works. It therefore seems likely that different decoration techniques were employed by these two firms.

In most cases actual ferns were used either directly or indirectly, although one process was a virtual copy of tartan ware, fern-printed

paper being used with the tell-tale gold wavy lines disguising joins on curved surfaces. The majority of fern ware, however, appears to involve the application of various types of fern to the wooden surface, which was then subjected to a dark brown stipple treatment before the removal of the ferns and subsequent varnishing.

While transfer and photographic wares were clearly intended for the souvenir trade this can hardly be said of fern ware. Even tartan ware is essentially Scottish, but since ferns occur in many parts of Britain articles in this group

Fern ware spherical wool holder on three bun feet. The diameter is 3⅞ inches (10 cm).

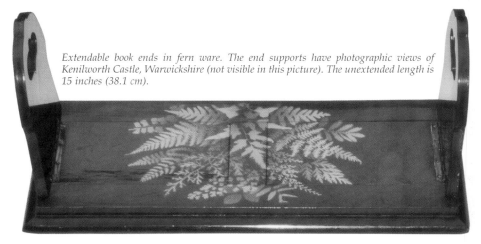

Extendable book ends in fern ware. The end supports have photographic views of Kenilworth Castle, Warwickshire (not visible in this picture). The unextended length is 15 inches (38.1 cm).

Left: *Fern ware plate, 8¼ inches (20.9 cm) in diameter, with the Nasmyth portrait of Robert Burns in the centre. This item is marked 'A Brown & Co. Patent', indicating that it was made at the Caledonian Box Works in Lanark.*

Right: *Tulip-shaped fern ware spill vase, 9 inches (22.8 cm) high.*

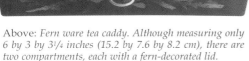

Above: *Fern ware tea caddy. Although measuring only 6 by 3 by 3¼ inches (15.2 by 7.6 by 8.2 cm), there are two compartments, each with a fern-decorated lid.*

This beautiful example of fern ware protects a copy of 'The National Melodist', a book of music published by William P. Nimmo of Edinburgh. It measures 10¼ by 8 inches (26 by 20.3 cm).

would simply have been bought for their undoubted visual appeal. However, some items of fern ware will be found either with an applied photograph or else with a cartouche stating the name of the place of purchase. Fortunately, few examples received this treatment, which hardly contributed to their general appearance.

Although fern ware was a relatively late introduction, a remarkably wide range of wares will be found in this decorative form. Full-size pieces of furniture such as chests of drawers, wardrobes and tables were also produced in fern ware but whether these were made in south-west Scotland or elsewhere is not known.

This delightful fern ware fan was almost certainly made for the French market.

36

Coloured fern and sea-flower ware

While coloured fern ware and sea-flower ware could be dealt with separately, they are visually so similar that separation might cause confusion. Neither of these finishes was recognised as a distinct Mauchline finish until the latter years of the twentieth century. A quick glance at the photograph below shows just how similar the two finishes are. Both forms of decoration are applied to plain sycamore and both are coloured primarily in shades of green and red. It is sometimes difficult even for an expert to decide to which of the categories some pieces should be ascribed.

Both finishes are very appealing, and since they usually adorn quite small items they make an excellent subject for a collection in their own right. However, you will sometimes find on sea-flower ware a unique characteristic not shared by fern ware, and it is this characteristic that gives it its name. Occasionally, in very small print, the following verse appears:

> Oh! call us not weeds, we are flowers of the sea,
> For lovely and bright, and gay tinted are we,
> And quite independent of sunshine or showers,
> Then call us not weeds, we are ocean's gay flowers!

The top photograph on page 10 includes a sea-flower decorated card case with this verse on the reverse side.

The mounted drum on stand (top centre) is a dispenser for string or possibly cotton and is in coloured fern decoration. The three lower items are in the same finish and are (from left to right) a circular pin disc, a round pin tray and a court plaster case ('plaister' in old Scottish spelling). The egg-shaped etui, the napkin ring in which it rests, and the tub-shaped money box are in sea-flower decoration.

Black lacquer ware

In 1861 Great Britain was plunged into mourning following the death of Prince Albert, Queen Victoria's consort. It seems highly likely that the large quantity of Mauchline ware produced with a black lacquer finish relates to this happening, with production continuing for the next forty years until Queen Victoria's own death in 1901.

In all cases the black lacquer finish was relieved with a more colourful addition, this often taking the form of a transfer-printed or

photographic view in a floral surround. Other examples carry sentimental verses, while a number of smaller boxes have been recorded with typical Welsh scenes such as the Welsh wedding, which, appropriately for a Welsh subject, is enhanced with a spray of lily of the valley.

Swivel note tablet with a transfer view of Bonchurch Pond, Isle of Wight.

Swivel note tablet with a transfer view of High Street, Lymington, Hampshire.

Black lacquer box depicting a Welsh wedding, with a floral spray of lily of the valley.

Small box with a transfer view of Ramsgate Harbour, Kent, with a floral spray.

Right: Cotton-reel holder (for six reels) combined with the game of fortunes. The decoration is in the form of a verse ('Friendship'), within a framework of flowers. The lower illustration of the open box shows the barrels at either end, containing a series of questions and answers. By spinning the side knobs, different questions and answers will appear in the slots visible in the upper photograph of the box with the lid closed.

Cylindrical box, possibly for toothpicks, with a transfer view of the Winter Gardens, Cheltenham, Gloucestershire. This structure was demolished in the 1940s.

Small box with a transfer view of Market Place, Nottingham, with a floral spray.

Black lacquer is generally restricted to smaller items such as boxes for all manner of purposes, swivel note tablets and sewing tools. However, examples for many other uses will be found, the combination of cotton-reel box and game of fortunes being just one. Other black lacquer pieces will be seen in group illustrations elsewhere in this book.

It is not known whether or not this box had a specific purpose, but the odd illustration suggests that it may have had. The 'horse' leading what appears to be a race of boneshaker bicycles could simply be a play on the phrase 'a one-horse race'.

Notebook with brass clasp and integral pencil. It bears a transfer view of Tunstall Hill and St Nicholas Church. Only the letters 'Su' are visible, but this is almost certainly Sunderland in County Durham.

Commemorative ware

Coronations and jubilees were too good an opportunity to be missed by the Smiths and their contemporaries. Queen Victoria's Golden Jubilee in 1887 and the coronation of George V in 1911 resulted in a number of commemorative items, although Victoria's Diamond Jubilee in 1897 seems to have been less well represented (possibly because of the Queen's age at the time and the fact that Mauchline ware itself was past its heyday by this date).

Left: *Jubilee pen wiper in, very appropriately, Victoria tartan.*

Below: *Lid of a small sewing box. The sides have transfer-printed views of the royal houses.*

Left and right: *Golden Jubilee paper knife. One side of the knife has Queen Victoria's portrait, along with information on all the members of the royal family. The reverse lists major events during Victoria's reign, the dates of all the Parliaments and the names of the Prime Ministers during the first fifty years of the Victorian era.*

King George V., born June 3, 1865.
Queen Mary, born May 26, 1867.
Married July 6, 1893.

ROYAL FAMILY.
Edward, Prince of Wales, born June 23, 1894.
Prince Albert, born December 14, 1895.
Princess Victoria, born April 25, 1897.
Prince Henry, born March 31, 1900.
Prince George, born December 20, 1902.
Prince John, born July 12, 1905.

Left: *The centre portion of an otherwise plain box, probably marking the coronation of George V and Queen Mary in 1911.*

Above: *Circular box, probably a powder container, with a fine transfer-printed view of the 1886 International Exhibition held in Edinburgh.*

Left: *Napkin rings were often produced in numbered sets of four or six and usually boxed. Many singletons were also made. The four rings illustrated here are numbered 2, 4, 5 and 6.*

This box is fitted as a small portable sewing companion. Its transfer decoration marks the meeting in 1871 of Dr David Livingstone and the American journalist Henry M. Stanley.

Above: *These two 'star' winders, with their seasonal messages, would make excellent presents for a keen needlewoman.*

Other notable occasions such as the International Exhibition held in Edinburgh in 1886 and the historic meeting of Dr David Livingstone and Henry M. Stanley on 10th November 1871 were also recognised. Livingstone was born at Blantyre, in South Lanarkshire, so he was almost a 'local' to the Ayrshire boxmakers.

Christmas was another time of opportunity and items carrying seasonal messages were made in large quantities.

Above: *Bezique scorer doubling as a Christmas gift. The scoring pins (one red and one white) are housed in purpose-made holes in the top edge of the scorer, held in by a swivel plate similar to the cribbage scorers on page 10.*

The export market

William and Andrew Smith of Mauchline and probably one or two other manufacturers enjoyed an extensive export trade, France being the most important European customer. Smiths employed a Paris agent and manufactured some items, including fans, exclusively for the French market. Many French locations, notably Nice and Boulogne, as well as some in Holland,

Memphremagog House, Newport, Vermont, United States. Built as a hotel in 1851 and later enlarged so that by 1863 it could accommodate four hundred guests. Notable among these was Prince Arthur, Duke of Connaught. This view is on a stamp box with two compartments.

Right: *Napkin ring, 2⅞ inches (7.5 cm) in diameter, with a transfer print of 'Matelote', Calais, France. The caption possibly relates to the seamanlike attire of the lady portrayed.*

Below: *Two napkin rings, decorated with indistinct photographs. (Left) Lions Head and Signal Hill, Cape Town, South Africa, showing the Drill Hall and Town Hall. (Right) Dunlop Street, Barrie; this is probably Barrie in Ontario, Canada. It is interesting that there appears to be an Edwardian motor car in the foreground, as very few motor vehicles have been recorded on Mauchline ware.*

Above: *A transfer-printed view of St James Hotel, Jacksonville, Florida, United States. The circular box holds a compass.*

Three transfer-printed French scenes. (Top left) This box, with a view of Biarritz, is tin-lined, suggesting use as a snuff container or similar. (Lower left) Notebook with metal clasp and original pencil, bearing a view of the Boulevard de la Croisette, Cannes. (Right) Another notebook with metal clasp and pencil; the view is of the 'Palais de Fontainebleau, Courdes Adieux'.

Belgium and even Spain have been recorded with transfer views. The British Empire was an obvious market and Mauchline ware was exported to South Africa, Canada and Australia as well as in large quantities to the United States. It seems likely that the development of some of these markets was associated with emigration from Scotland during the second half of the nineteenth century. The Australian market is thought to have resulted from the emigration of Andrew Smith's daughter shortly after her marriage in 1858.

A notebook with pencil and metal clasp. The view is of Bourke Street, Melbourne, Victoria, Australia.

Above: *Purse with a transfer-printed view of 'Fontaine des Elephants', Chambéry, about 55 miles (88 km) east-south-east of Lyons, France.*

Transfer-printed view of Mokoia Island, which lies within Lake Rotoruo on New Zealand's North Island. The area is noted for its very hot springs. Views of New Zealand are quite rare.

Buying, selling and collecting

Mauchline ware covers an enormous range of items, in numerous finishes, and anyone planning to start a collection will need to consider carefully whether to collect every type of Mauchline ware possible or whether a specialised collection might give equal, or even greater, satisfaction. The latter course could well be less costly.

A limited collection would clearly take longer to assemble, but perhaps this is a good thing. Searching is much of the fun. A large number of related items can also be visually quite stunning. There are collectors who limit themselves to fern ware or tartan ware only. An attempt to collect an example of each of the recorded tartans would be a real test of endurance and may never be achieved in one lifetime!

One might decide to collect a particular product such as napkin rings or egg cups, both of which were made in very large numbers. Another possibility is to specialise in transfer-printed and/or photographic items of a particular geographical location or subject. One collector is known to have assembled more than 150 views of seaside piers! The possibilities are endless but if you do take the plunge, be prepared to become hooked. It certainly will not harm your health, but it may well dent your pocket...

Buying Mauchline ware has become more difficult simply because so many very large collections have been amassed. However, from time to time collections are sold for one reason or another and these usually find their way to a specialist auction house. Several large collections have been sold through Bruton Knowles of Gloucester (in which firm the well known antiques personality Arthur Negus was a partner) at their Cheltenham Auction Rooms. Some of the illustrations in this book relate to these auctions and are reproduced with their permission. Other auction houses have also handled large collections.

There are several specialist Mauchline ware dealers but any dealer in small antiques may have a few pieces. Thus any one of the many antiques markets and regular antiques fairs held in most parts of Britain could prove to be a happy hunting ground. Joining the Mauchline Ware Collectors Club (MWCC) is essential if you want to take collecting seriously. Specialist dealers advertise in the club's thrice-yearly journal, which is available only to club members. The club's address is printed opposite.

Selling Mauchline ware is simply a reverse process. Auction houses or dealers are the main outlets, along with the MWCC members' convention that takes place every eighteen months or so and includes opportunities to buy and sell as well as the chance to see other members' collections.

This unusual item, a tankard 2¼ inches (6 cm) high, was produced from a block of alternately contrasting light and dark woods. It has a coloured fern decoration. Other objects using this construction method have been recorded.

Places to visit

It is important to remember that most museums in the United Kingdom have far more items in their collections than can possibly be displayed at any one time. It can be very frustrating to visit a museum expecting to see a known (or suspected) Mauchline ware collection only to find that no items are on view. It would, therefore, be prudent to make enquiries before embarking upon such visits. Many museums do have Mauchline ware in their collections, some holding just a few items and others with large displays.

Large collections
Abbey House Museum, Abbey Walk, Kirkstall, Leeds LS5 3EH. Telephone: 0113 230 5492. Website: www.leeds.gov.uk/abbeyhouse (Includes the Gwen Harrison bequest.)
Baird Institute, Lugar Street, Cumnock, Ayrshire KA18 1AD. Telephone: 01290 421701.
Birmingham Museum and Art Gallery, Chamberlain Square, Birmingham B3 3DH. Telephone: 0121 303 2834. Website: www.bmag.org.uk (Houses the well known Pinto Collection.)
Burns House Museum, Castle Street, Mauchline, Ayrshire KA5 5BZ. Telephone: 01290 550045. Website: www.east-ayrshire.gov.uk
Museum of Barnstaple and North Devon, The Square, Barnstaple, North Devon EX32 8LN. Telephone: 01271 346747. Website: www.devon.gov.uk
Royal Museum of Scotland, Chambers Street, Edinburgh EH1 1JF. Telephone: 0131 247 4219. Website: www.nms.ac.uk

Small collections
The museums listed below have collections of transfer and photographic ware relating to their locality.
Cheltenham Art Gallery and Museum, Clarence Street, Cheltenham, Gloucestershire GL50 3JT. Telephone: 01242 237431. Website: www.cheltenhammuseum.org.uk
Hastings Museum and Art Gallery, John's Place, Bohemia Road, Hastings, Sussex TN34 1ET. Telephone: 01424 781155. Website: www.hmag.org.uk
Towner Art Gallery and Museum, High Street, Old Town, Eastbourne, East Sussex BN20 8BB. Telephone: 01323 411688. Website: www.eastbourne.org/entertainment

---

Further reading

Many books on general antiques include some reference to Mauchline ware but those listed below are dedicated solely to this subject.

Furstenberg, Princess Ira von. *Tartanware: Souvenirs from Scotland*. Pavilion Books, 1997.
Pinto, E. H. and E. R. *Tunbridge and Scottish Souvenir Woodware*. Bell, 1970. Unfortunately now out of print.
Trachtenburg, David, and Keith, Thomas. *Mauchline Ware: A Collector's Guide*. Antique Collectors' Club, 2002.

Mauchline Ware Collectors Club (MWCC)
Formed in 1986, this club has many hundreds of members based largely in the United Kingdom and the United States but also in other countries. It publishes a journal every four months and organises members' conventions at regular intervals. Information about the MWCC can be obtained by post (PO Box 158, Leeds LS16 5WZ); via the website (www.mauchlinewareclub.co.uk); or by email (enquiries@mauchlinewareclub.org).

Index

This index lists people, firms and locations referred to in the text and the lengthier captions of this book.

An advertisement from 'Menzies' Tourist Pocket Guide for Scotland', 1852. Note the wide range of plane tree (sycamore) items, now referred to as Mauchline ware, available at the time from S. Woolfield of 61 Buchanan Street, Glasgow.